I SPOT TRIANGLES

T0100304

first concepts

Triangles are everywhere!
The sign is a triangle.

The hanger is a triangle.

5

The sandwich is
a triangle.

The pizza is a triangle.

The sail is a triangle.

The tree is a triangle.

13

The house is a triangle.

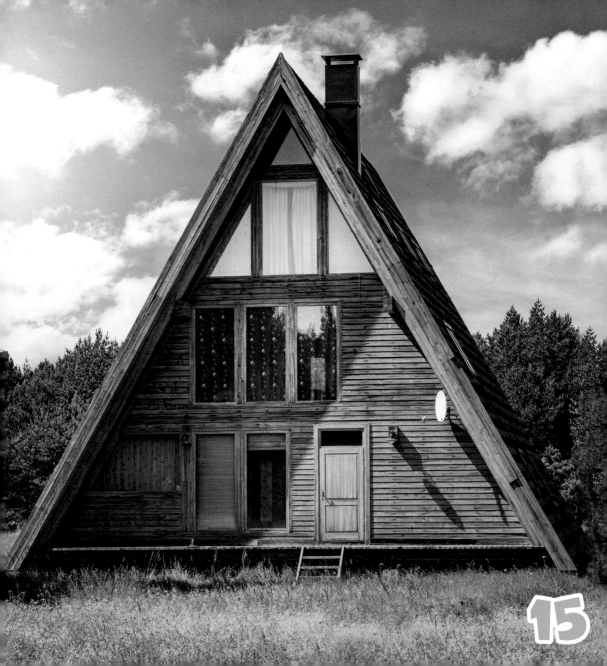

15

The flag is a triangle.

17

The mountain is
a triangle.

The chip is a triangle.

21

Can you spot
the triangle?

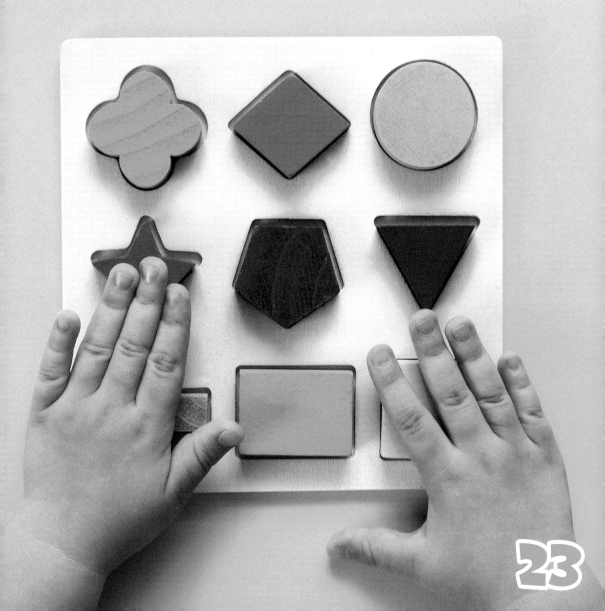

Please visit our website, www.garethstevens.com. For a free color catalog of all our high-quality books, call toll free 1-800-542-2595 or fax 1-877-542-2596.

Library of Congress Cataloging-in-Publication Data
Names: Humphrey, Natalie, author.
Title: I spot triangles / Natalie Humphrey.
Description: Buffalo, New York : Gareth Stevens Publishing, [2025] |
    Series: I spot shapes | Includes index.
Identifiers: LCCN 2023044386 (print) | LCCN 2023044387 (ebook) | ISBN
    9781538291832 (library binding) | ISBN 9781538291825 (paperback) | ISBN
    9781538291849 (ebook)
Subjects: LCSH: Triangle–Juvenile literature. | Shapes–Juvenile
    literature.
Classification: LCC QA482 .H863 2025 (print) | LCC QA482 (ebook) | DDC
    516/.154–dc23/eng/20231023
LC record available at https://lccn.loc.gov/2023044386
LC ebook record available at https://lccn.loc.gov/2023044387

Published in 2025 by
Gareth Stevens Publishing
2544 Clinton Street
West Seneca, NY 14224

Copyright © 2025 Gareth Stevens Publishing

Designer: Leslie Taylor
Editor: Natalie Humphrey

Photo credits: Cover (sky) Andi Alif Wijaya/Shutterstock.com, (flags) New Africa/Shutterstock.com;
p. 3 Vladfotograf/Shutterstock.com; p. 5 Calypso Photo/Shutterstock.com; p. 7 Elena..D/Shutterstock.com;
p. 9 bestv/Shutterstock.com; p. 11 Michal Balada/Shutterstock.com; p. 13 Maram/Shutterstock.com;
p. 15 Valdis Skudre/Shutterstock.com; p. 17 Thomas Pajot/Shutterstock.com; p. 19 Kiwisoul/
Shutterstock.com; p. 21 vitals/Shutterstock.com; p. 23 MariaKa/Shutterstock.com.

Printed in the United States of America

CPSIA compliance information: Batch #CSGS25: For further information contact Gareth Stevens, New York, New York at 1-800-542-2595.